If Only
I Could Fly

*Poems for Kids
to Read Out Loud*

by Brod Bagert

Illustrated by Stephen Morillo

Published by

Juliahouse Publishers
815 Baronne St.
New Orleans, Louisiana 70113

Design by Stephen Morillo.
The poems are set in Century Book,
the heads in Bookman Medium.

First Edition
ISBN 0-9614228-0-7

DEDICATION

Dedicated with love to my children Jennifer, Colette and Brody, and to my wife Debby, who somehow manages to mother the four of us.

Table of Contents

Author's Note i

Mean Teachers 1
Next Week's Angel 2
No 4
If Only I Could Fly 7
Caterpillars 8
The Fight At Little Recess 10
Little League Magic 13
The Night I Caught The Burglars 15
Empty Promises 16
The Time I Learned To Ride My Bike 18
The Bad Mood Bug 20
First Place Medal 22
Sunday Snail 24
A Goblin In My Throat 27
Country Grandmother 28
Winnifred's Secret 30
Milk 33
Lost And Found 35
The Time Irving Got Mad 36
Day Time Sleepers 38
Crazy Daddy 41
Ozark Oscar 42
Split Pants 44
Homework 45
Autumn's Witch 46
Yesterday's Magnolia 49
Thank You Prayer 51
The Day That I Grow Old 53

The Author 55
The Illustrator 55

AUTHOR'S NOTE

These poems are specifically written to be read out loud by children. They are designed to help children create a dramatic interpretation, not just a reading.

It all started on April Fool's Day of 1981. My wife Debby was trying to select a poem for our 7 year old to recite in the school elocution contest, and she was having a hard time. It seemed that much of the available material, although fun and entertaining, simply did not recite well. The words seemed to lose believability when read by a child. Colette's first performance would be difficult enough, butterflies and all, and her mother wanted her to have material that would help her do well.

In the tradition of hectic political campaigns, I arrived home at about 3 a.m. from a production session at a local television station and found Debby sitting on the floor amid a scatter of books. She explained that she had been unable to find a suitable poem and asked if I would write one. I did. Later that morning Colette submitted the poem *The Night I Caught the Burglars*, with which she eventually earned 2nd place in the school competition.

Four days later I lost the election for a full term on the Louisiana Public Service Commission, retired from active political life, and began to rediscover my children. It was the beginning of a wonderful time during which I wrote these poems about the fun, fear, silliness, challenge and sorrow of childhood.

Since that time, my own children and their classmates have performed these poems at various functions and competitions. We've had a lot of fun with them and offer them to you in the hope you will enjoy them as well.

A special thanks to Gail & Pete Rizzo, Charlotte Rivet, Lea Young and Gary Esolen for their suggestions and encouragement. Thanks also to the talented production staff of Metro 4 Graphics: Teresa Askew, Jackie Miller, Beth Eigher, Lisa Morillo, Nick Marinello and Tony Vasconcellos.

Mean Teachers

I'm standing in the corner
'Cuz my teacher is a ghoul.
Every time I have some fun
She claims I broke a rule.

When I grow up I'll show her.
I'll teach her two plus two.
When I make the rules
I'll close all the schools
And I'll lock her in the zoo.

Next Week's Angel

Monday night I fibbed to Mom.

Tuesday I was better.

Wednesday I slipped up again
I read my sister's letter.
It was mushy muck and lovey talk
And smoochy smoochy goo,
What fun... until she caught me
And whacked me with her shoe.

Thursday I played after dark.

Friday was a bummer.
I filled the toilet with red paint
And flushed it on the plumber.

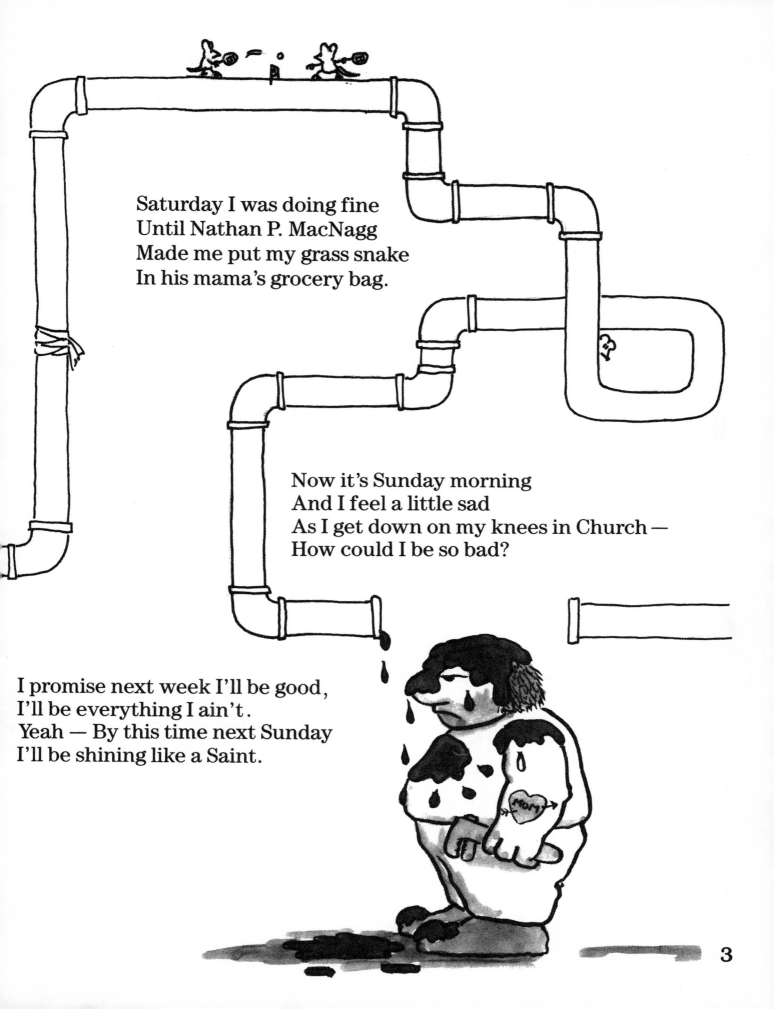

Saturday I was doing fine
Until Nathan P. MacNagg
Made me put my grass snake
In his mama's grocery bag.

Now it's Sunday morning
And I feel a little sad
As I get down on my knees in Church —
How could I be so bad?

I promise next week I'll be good,
I'll be everything I ain't.
Yeah — By this time next Sunday
I'll be shining like a Saint.

3

NO

You'll hear it every day
It's how they teach the rules.

"NO, you cannot stay in bed today
Get up and dress for school."

NO, you'll have to wait for recess.

NO, don't bite your nails.

NO, the lunch room's not the place
To braid your pony tails.

NO you can't go out to play.

NO cookies.

NO ice cream.

NO, it's time for homework.

It's enough to make you scream.

They sure do like that NO
They use it day and night.
I just wish I could teach them
The way to use it right.

NO need to make your bed today.

NO homework for a week.

NO more chores.

NO locked doors.

NO time when kids can't speak.

NO nasty don'ts.

NO never do's.

NO Sunday clothes.

NO leather shoes.

It's not a bad word after all
If you don't abuse it.
It all depends whose mouth it's in
And how they're gonna use it.

If Only I Could Fly

If only I could fly
If only I were magic
I would soar into the sky.
Oh I would be so happy
I'd never ever cry —
If only only only if
If only I could fly.

Caterpillars

They came like dew drops overnight
Eating every plant in sight,
Those nasty worms with legs that crawl
So creepy up the garden wall,
Green prickly fuzz to hurt and sting
Each unsuspecting living thing.
How I hate them! Oh, you know
I'd love to squish them with my toe.
But then I see past their disguise,
Someday they'll all be butterflies.

The Fight at Little Recess

He pushed me
In front of all my friends,
He told me I was chicken.
So I said, "That all depends."

They laughed at me, I could have died,
I was about to cry.
Oh please no tears, do something quick —
So I punched him in his eye.

We rolled and kicked and twisted arms
From the sidewalk to the grass
Until the bell began to ring —
At last! It was time to go to class.

He figured he could pick on me
But I sure gave him a whirl.
The fool thought I'd be scared to fight
Just 'cuz I'm a girl.

Little League Magic

I got a hit each time at bat
(It was the rabbit's foot inside my hat).

I stole a base, slid safe at home
(Today I used my broken comb).

My glove was hot on every play
(I didn't wash my socks today).

But now I feel real scary
With a creepy kind of horror—
Oh sure I played OK today
But will my magic work tomorrow?

The Night I Caught the Burglars

Last night I heard a funny noise
While I was in my bed
And thought, should I get up and take a peek
Or go back to sleep instead.

Up I got, feet on the floor
As quiet as a mouse.
And made my way from room to room
Throughout the darkened house.

Then I saw them, tall and mean
In the middle of the night
Two men were stuffing all my toys
Into a sack and out of sight.

I jumped right out and shouted stop!
I pushed them to the floor.
I held them 'til the policemen came
And led them out the door.

It felt so nice to be so brave,
My Mom and Dad were beaming.
But then the clock began to ring —
Oh shucks! I was just dreaming.

Empty Promises

Please Honeybee
Don't sting me.
I won't steal the honey
From your hollow tree.

Won't you trust me?
I'll make you glad
To learn that people
Are not all bad.

Wow! That honey was just great!
I know I shouldn't lie
But it tastes so good I can't resist
No matter how I try.

The Time I Learned to Ride My Bike

My Daddy said, "Today's the day
You're going to learn to ride."
So I ran upstairs into my room
To find a place to hide.

But now I'm sitting on this bike
No training wheels in sight.
How did he talk me into this?
I sure hope he was right.

I feel the pedals turn.
I start to move real slow.
What if I fall and break my arm?
"Oh Daddy! Please don't let me go!"

His hands are gone — I'm doing it
Much longer than I dared.
It's not so hard, it's kind of fun
Now why was I so scared?

I was just great — they cheered for me
My Daddy didn't lie.
If you want to ride a bike
You just get on and try.

The Bad Mood Bug

I don't know what I want today
But nothing feels quite right.
If I had an ice cream pie
I wouldn't take a bite.

I wouldn't ride a water slide
Or climb a monkey tree.
No games, no toys, no magic wands,
No elephants for me.

I believe deep down inside me
There sleeps a grouchy bug
Who wakes up every now and then
And makes me feel like crud.

First Place Medal

They cheered so loud
I felt so proud
My chest began to swell,

I grew and I puffed and I bloated —

Then to my disgrace
It spread up to my face!

It never stopped
and then......
        I POPPED!

For a while it was nice to be a winner

But now I'm relaxed

And my head's a lot thinner.

The Sunday Snail

I see you slimy slow-poke snail
As you leave your silky silver trail
Sliding over rocks and grass
Your eyes on poles, your shell like glass.

I cannot stay here all day long
You move so slow, is something wrong?
I'd like to know where you will go
But Alas! I'm late for Mass.

There's A Goblin In My Throat

There's a Goblin in my throat
And he's such a nasty goat
He plays tricks with the words that I speak.
I try to say "clown"
And it changes to "frown".
This morning I whispered
"Sunshine and Flowers"
And it came out instead
"Mad dogs and howlers."

It's very hard to sound cheerful

With a goblin in your throat

But still I lov...hate...

Because life is so beautif...ugly...

You see what I mean?

Country Grandmother

Our Grandma's in the country
And you'd think she loves to cook,
To make thick fudge and apple pie
In a rocking chair with failing eyes,
Smiling sweet, hair silver grey
You'd think she knits and sews all day.

Well—you'd be wrong.
She hates to cook.
No fudge, no peaceful time to sew
Because she's always on the go.

This Grandma jogs at the crack of dawn
and cuts her own two-acre lawn.
Reads current books
Attends college classes
Wears rhinestones in bi-focal glasses.
Although today she's seventy
And forever on the run,
She says when she's one hundred
She'll really have some fun.

Winifred's Secret

At school they wouldn't play with her
She hadn't been there very long
And everything she tried to do
Seemed to turn out wrong.

She spent lunchtime sitting on a swing
Alone — all knots inside
And after she got home
She fell across her bed and cried.

"I hate that school," she told her mom,
"I won't go back again...
You just don't know how bad it feels
To live without a friend."

Her momma said "I love you Winifred
No matter what you do
But I'll tell you of a secret
That I've come to learn is true.
If you want to, you'll find happiness
In a worn out leather shoe...
Or else you'll find it nowhere,
It's completely up to you."

She went back to school
She studied hard
She struggled through the worst
And found that she made lots of friends
When she put their feelings first.

She didn't try to boss them
Or always be the best
And the rest it seemed came easily —
She was past her hardest test.

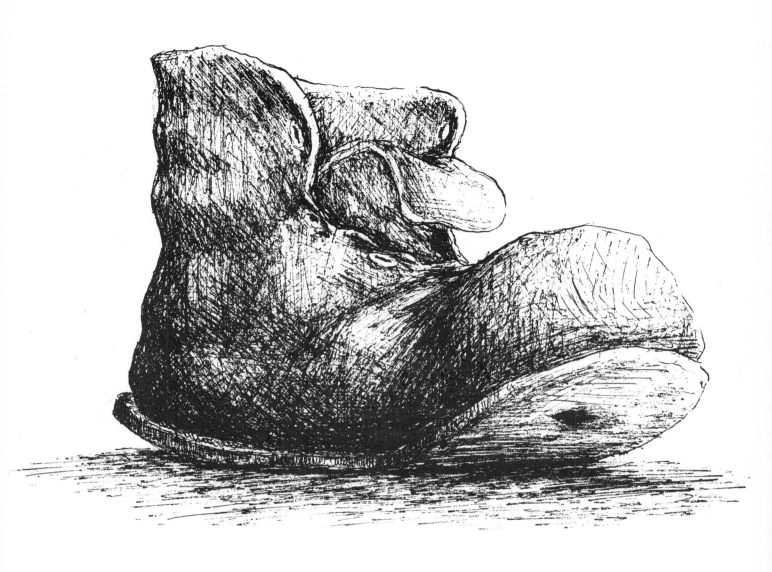

She lived 'till she was ninety-six
And on the day she died
She called her great-great-grand kids
To sit down at her side.
She said "I love you all my children
No matter what you do
And I'll tell you of a secret
I've come to learn is true.
If you want to, you'll find happiness
In a worn out leather shoe…
Or else you'll find it nowhere,
It's completely up to you."

Milk

I love my milk at breakfast
On rice crispies or corn flakes
Or when my Mom puts chocolate in
And ice cream to make shakes.

I love it cold at supper
And when night things start to creep
I like it nice and warm in bed
To help me go to sleep.

It's not like Coke or 7-up.
They make it white
But I'm not sure how.
All I know for certain is
They start off with a cow.

Lost And Found

There he is!
He looked this way
He's smiling and he sees me.
Oh boy I'm found
Swept off the ground
Please Dad, don't ever leave me.

Sure I get mad and fight with Dad
He always wants his way.
But right now snuggled in his arms
Is where I want to stay.

The Time Irving Got Mad

He got so mad he held his breath.
He got so mad he stubbed his toe.
He got so mad he ran away
But found there was no place to go.
So mad
He broke up all his toys
Tore his clothes, bonked his nose
Yelled and screamed the whole day long
And everything we did was wrong.
His friends called up
The neighbors came
The priest said prayers in Irving's name
Doctors poked and
Lawyers joked
But Irving's mood remained the same.
He stayed that way from May the 3rd
Until the 5th day of December
Till someone asked: "Why are you mad?"
Then Irving smiled.
"I don't remember."

Day Time Sleepers

My hamster snoozes all day long
And plays at night while I sleep.
What foolish hours to keep!
I tell him what's right
He should sleep at night
But in spite of my constant warning
At night he runs around in his wheel
And he goes to sleep in the morning.

Crazy Daddy

He carves faces on our pumpkins
Hangs out spider webs and ghosts
Tombstones, graves
And a sound that shocks us
As creatures crawl from long pine boxes.
He gives out lots of things to eat
To the kids who come to trick or treat
With a special growl if you're a scaredy —
Just another Halloween
With our crazy daddy.

Ozark Oscar

Ozark Oscar the mountain man
Had big red eyes and grizzly hands.
He wore his hair down to his shoulders
And cleaned his teeth on mountain boulders.
You could see him on the dirt back-roads
Eatin' blue-tailed skinks and puffy toads.
The mountain kids all knew his song
Oscar growled and howled and snorted all day long.
But once too often on his foggy hill
He drank corn squeezins from his whiskey still,
Went drunk to sleep and folks never dared
To wake him up — so don't be scared.

Split Pants

I did a handspring on the ground
And heard that awful tearing sound.
The girls began to giggle
The boys began to jeer
So I held my ears and closed my eyes
And tried to disappear.

Homework

I would have done it yesterday
If it weren't for the rain.
All that lightning and thunder
Are so tricky on the brain.

I'd like to work real hard tonight
To raise my grades right out of sight
But my finger has a splinter
And it's painful when I write.

Now I know you won't believe me,
But no matter what I do
It's tomorrow night for homework
And I promise that is true.

Autumn's Witch

When from the hidden hills of chalk
Creep dry whispers of the bone
Eye bulges from a knotted tree
Voices frozen in a stone,

When in the shadow of a vulture's w
A lonely gypsy band
Sees the fortune of an evil queen
In a veiled and wrinkled hand,

46

When a large and orange moon
Whirs its hollow melody
Through all the things that crackle
To all the souls that groan

Then to a graveyard you must go—
Or some other haunted place,
For Autumn's witch has come again
To spin her spider's lace.

47

Yesterday's Magnolia

I walked outside this morning
And saw a man climbing in my tree.
How nice that he would like
To do the same fun things as me.

But when I heard the chain saw growl
The tears rushed down my face
He was about to use it
To chop down my favorite place.

I yelled ''Wait!
Don't cut another branch!''
— Too late.
The only tree that I could reach
And now there's just a hole.

I feel so sad and angry
But I don't know who to blame.
No matter what you do in life
Nothing ever stays the same.

Thank You Prayer

Thank you for another day
To love
To work
To worship
And to play.
Thank you for these heartbeats
This breath
These precious hours.
Help me give love like your sun
And receive it like your flowers.

The Day That I Grow Old

When will it come?
How will I know the day that I grow old?
Will I have to give up fun
The minute I turn twenty-one?
Will all my friends turn mean and dirty
That dreadful day when I turn thirty?
Or does it come much later on?
With luck long after I am gone.

THE AUTHOR

Brod Bagert married his childhood sweetheart Debby Kerne and has three children: Jennifer, Colette and Brody.

He is a practicing trial lawyer and a well known figure in New Orleans political circles, which he once frequented as a member of the New Orleans City Council and as a Louisiana Public Service Commissioner.

Brod likes music. He has played the harmonica since childhood, taught himself guitar at 33 and began studying the violin at 35. He is building his own violin which he hopes to finish before senility sets in.

For exercise he swims, bicycles and runs. He loses 250 pounds a year or 1.6 pounds per diet, the average duration of which is 22 hours and 15 minutes.

He is a practicing Catholic, loves his family and is thankful for his friends.

THE ILLUSTRATOR

Stephen Morillo was born 26 years ago and began drawing soon thereafter. Horrified, his parents sent him to school to learn an honest trade. Instead, he started drawing cartoons. By high school, he was into the hard stuff — oil painting.

He had, however, also developed a keen interest in history. This led him first to Harvard, where he got a B.A. in medieval history, then to Oxford, where he wrote a D.Phil. dissertation on twelfth century English royal warfare. While in England, he also added rowing and cricket to the many sports he watches and enthusiastically (if unskillfully) plays.

Having concurrently pursued his artistic education, he felt it quite natural to take his Oxford degree and become a staff artist at the New Orleans weekly newspaper *Gambit*. He continues to paint. He is married to Lisa Wedig. He has no children, though Lisa does claim to take care of one large child.